ASK ISAAC ASIMOV ?

Why do stars twinkle?

Heinemann

First published in Great Britain by Heinemann Library
an imprint of Heinemann Publishers (Oxford) Ltd
Halley Court, Jordan Hill, Oxford OX2 8EJ

OXFORD LONDON EDINBURGH MADRID
ATHENS BOLOGNA PARIS MELBOURNE
SYDNEY AUCKLAND SINGAPORE TOKYO
IBADAN NAIROBI HARARE GABORONE
PORTSMOUTH NH (USA)

98 97 96 95 94

10 9 8 7 6 5 4 3 2 1

British Library Cataloguing in Publication Data is available from the British Library on request.

ISBN 0 431 07655 3

Cover designed and pages typeset by Philip Parkhouse
Printed in China

Picture Credits
Paul Dimare, pp. 8-9; Gareth Stevens, Inc., © 1989, p. 17 (inset); Paul H. Henning/Third Coast, © 1983; pp. 10-11; Rick Karpinski/DeWalt and Associates, pp. 4-5; © Fred Klein, pp. 18-19; Mark Maxwell, pp. 14-15; Mark Mille/DeWalt and Associates, pp. 12-13; NASA, pp. 6-7, 20-21; National Optical Astronomy Observatories, pp. 16-17, 24; © NRAO/AUI, p. 19 (inset); © Frank Zullo, pp. 22-23.

Cover photograph © Science Photo Library/David Nunuk
Back cover photograph © Sygma/D. Kirkland

Series editor: Elizabeth Kaplan
Editor: Kelli Peduzzi
Series designer: Sabine Huschke
Picture researcher: Daniel Helminak
Consulting editor: Matthew Groshek

Contents

Words that appear in the glossary are printed in **bold** the first time they occur in the text.

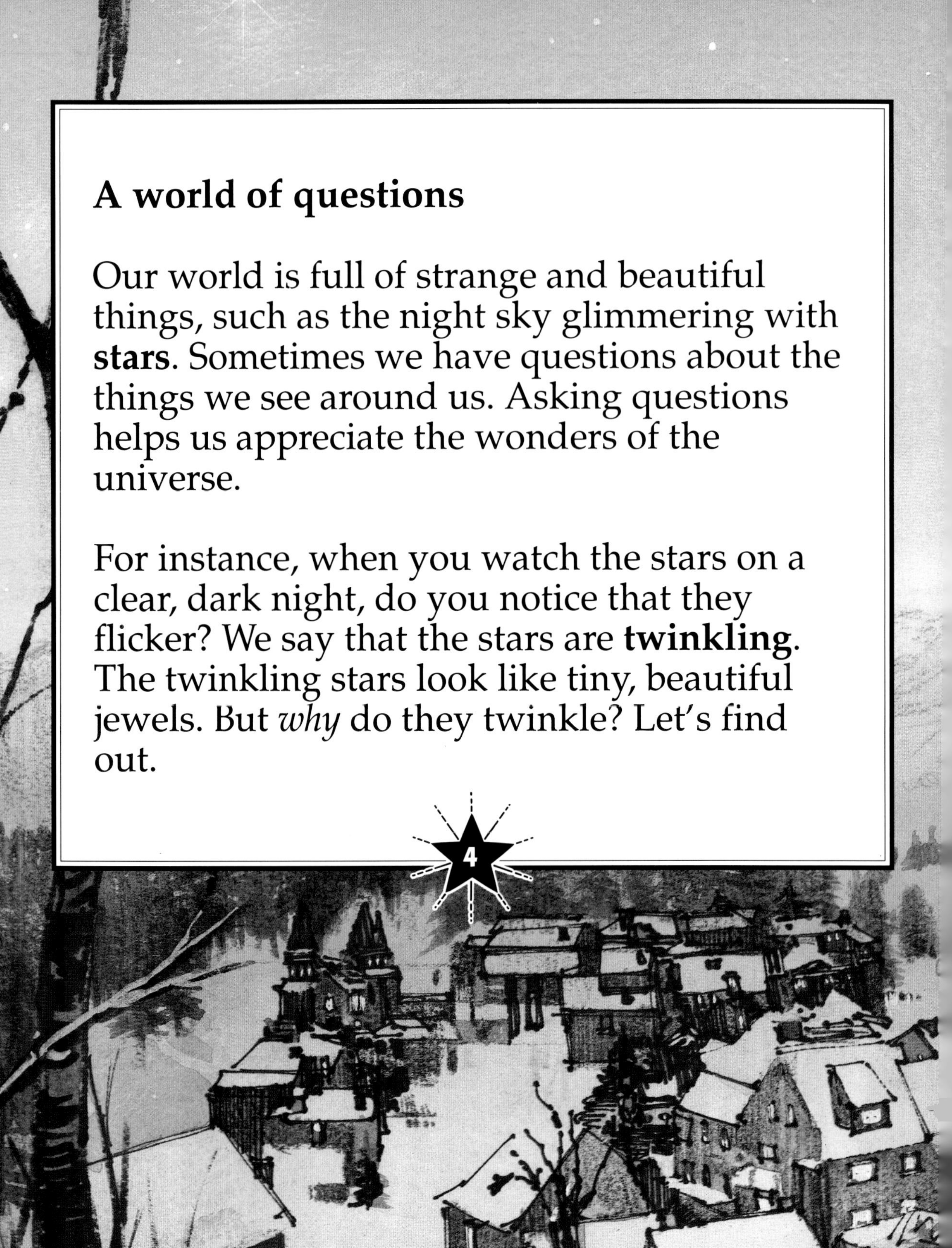

A world of questions

Our world is full of strange and beautiful things, such as the night sky glimmering with **stars**. Sometimes we have questions about the things we see around us. Asking questions helps us appreciate the wonders of the universe.

For instance, when you watch the stars on a clear, dark night, do you notice that they flicker? We say that the stars are **twinkling**. The twinkling stars look like tiny, beautiful jewels. But *why* do they twinkle? Let's find out.

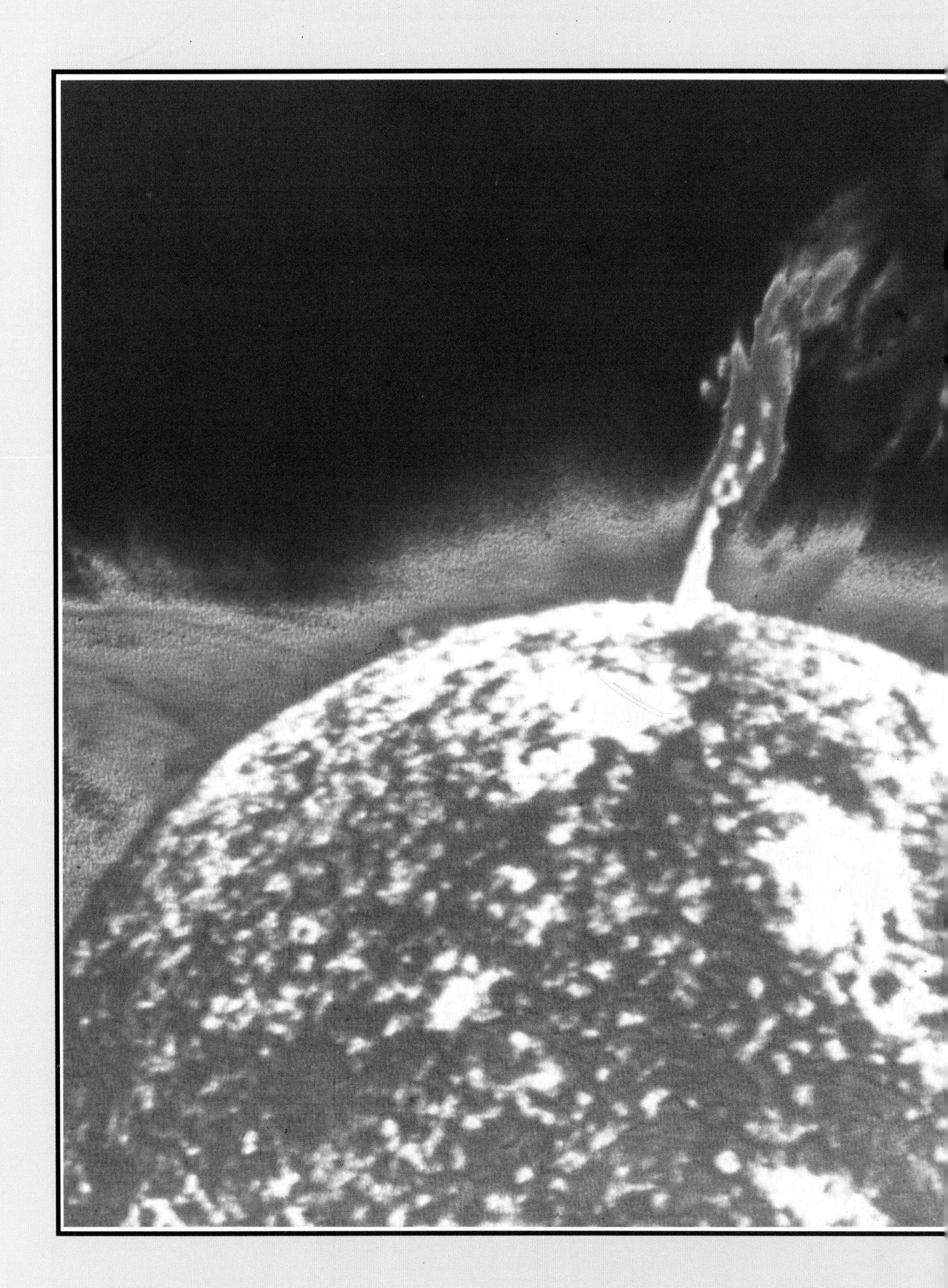

What are stars?

Stars are huge globes of hot gas. They send their light and heat out into space. The star nearest to us is the Sun. It is 150 million kilometres away. Yet it is close enough for us to feel its warmth.

The Sun is just an average-sized star. Yet to us, it looks like a huge disc of light in the sky. Compared to the Sun, other stars look like tiny specks of light.

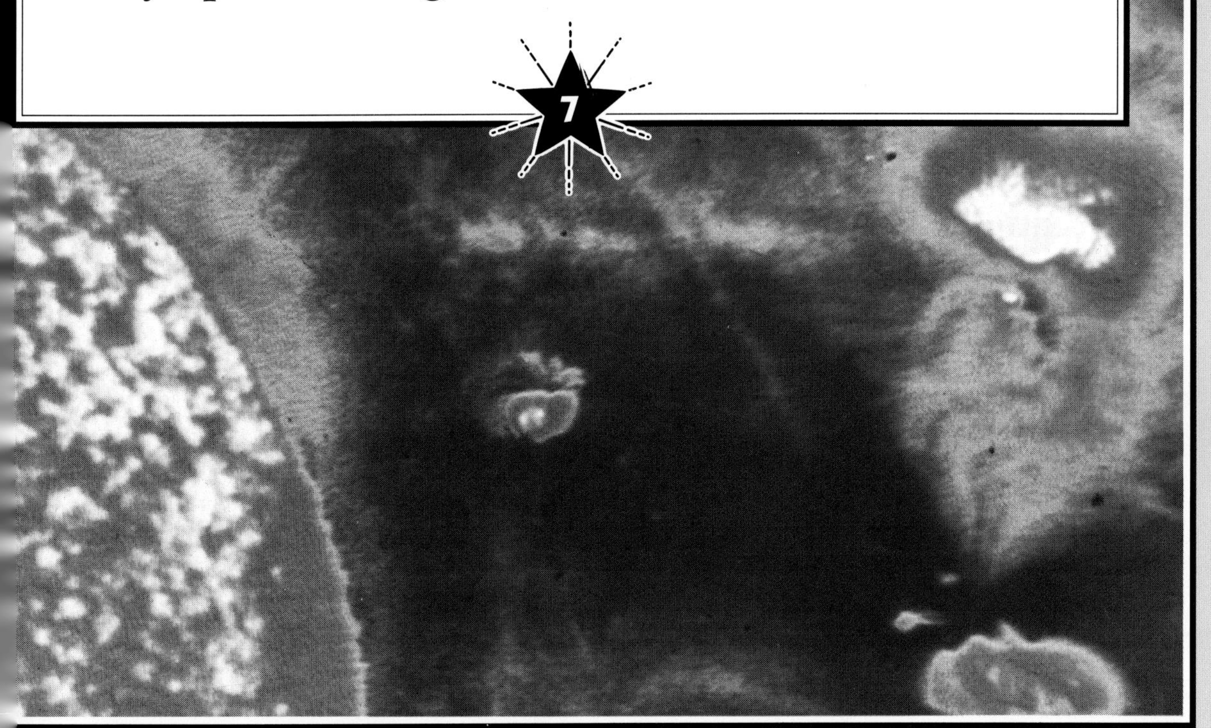

The faraway stars

Other stars are much further away from us than the Sun. They are so far away we see them only as tiny points of light. During the daytime, the bright light from the Sun drowns them out. We can see the other stars' light only at night.

The gleaming dot of light in this picture is how the Sun would look from the planet Pluto, shown here with its moon, Charon. From Pluto, the Sun would be too far away to brighten the sky or warm the planet.

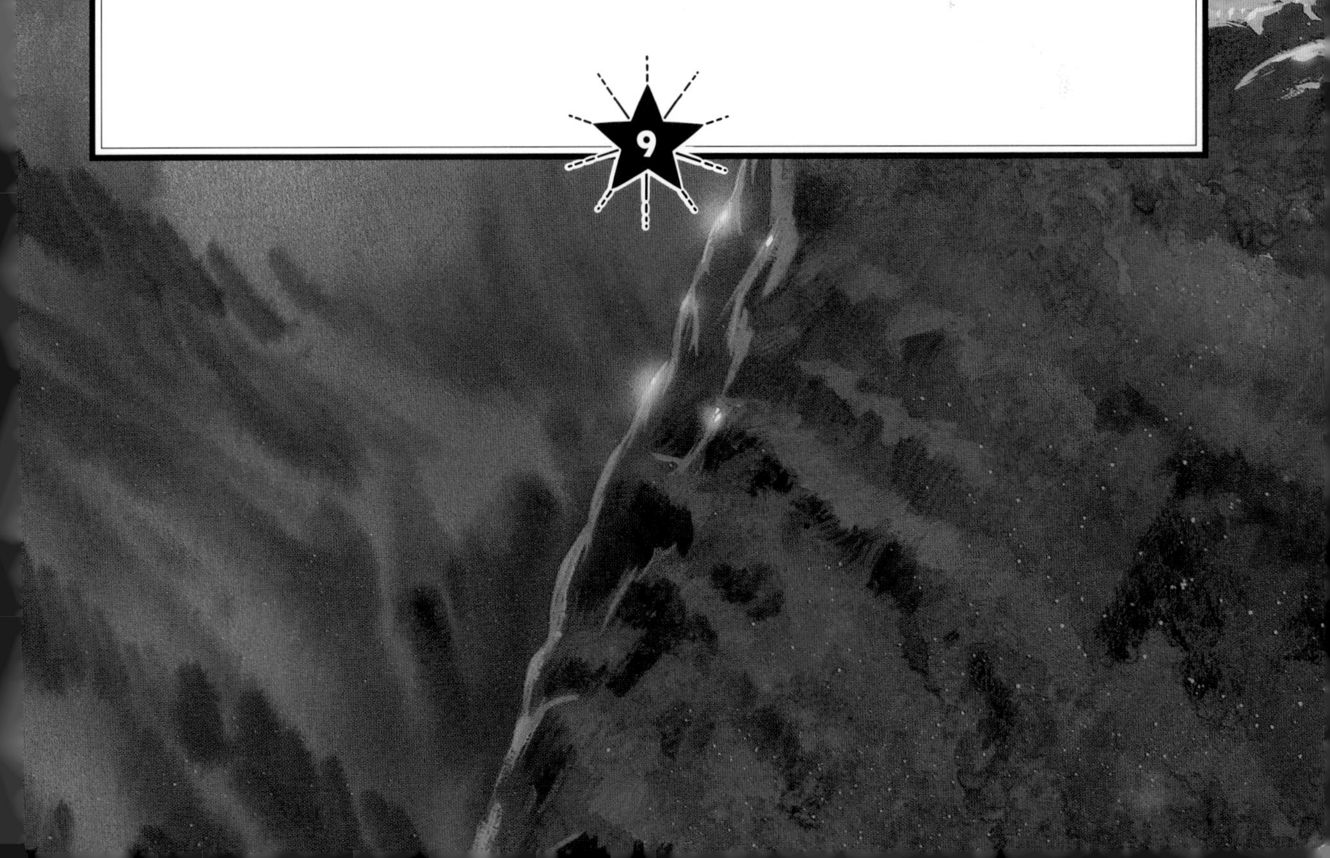

Do stars really twinkle?

Starlight comes straight to us from far away, but its long journey ends with strange twists and turns. In fact, twinkling stars are not really changing their brightness at all. They just look as if they are! Twinkling is an **optical illusion**, something that looks real but isn't.

We can see another optical illusion. As we travel along on a hot, sunny day, we may see what looks like water shimmering on the road ahead. But as we get closer, the water disappears. This optical illusion happens for the same reason that stars appear to twinkle.

How light travels

Shimmering road? Twinkling stars? Both of these optical illusions happen because of the way light travels. Most of the time, it travels in a straight line. But light will bend when it passes through layers of hot and cold air.

On warm days, the layers of air near the ground get hotter than the layers that are higher up. When light passes through the hot air and then through the cool air, it bends. To the eye, the bending light makes the road surface look as if it is rippling.

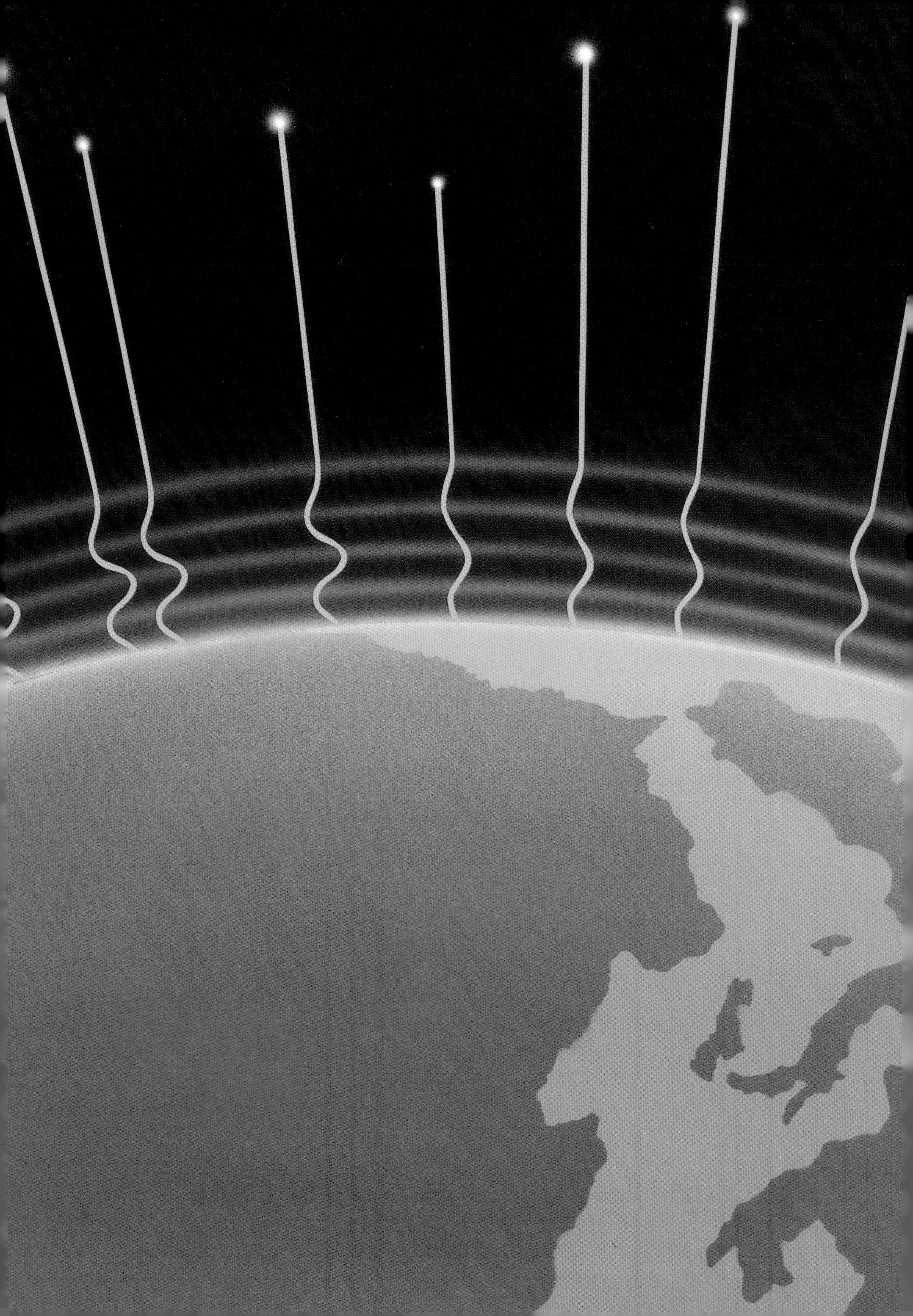

Why does starlight twinkle?

Starlight also passes through layers of hot and cold air in the Earth's atmosphere. As starlight passes through these layers, it bends. When we see the stars twinkling, what we really see is the starlight bending as it passes through the air.

Stars twinkle more in the early evening, when warm air rises from the ground. If you live in a place where day and night temperatures are very different, you will also see more twinkling.

Why is it difficult to look at stars?

Astronomers use **telescopes** to look at the stars. A telescope makes the stars look larger and brighter than they appear to the naked eye. An astronomer gets a closer look at the stars with a telescope, but the twinkling looks even stronger, too.

This makes stargazing tricky for astronomers. They want to be able to see the stars clearly, but the twinkling makes the stars fade in and out. Astronomers need the starlight to remain steady so that they can study the stars.

A clearer view of the stars

Astronomers have found ways to get a better look at the stars. To lessen the twinkling, they put telescopes high in the mountains, where the air is cold and clear. They also put telescopes near the ocean, where the day and night temperatures are fairly steady.

Astronomers also use computers to see the stars. A computer helps a telescope to focus on a star using special **lasers** and mirrors. The computer then takes what the telescope sees and turns it into pictures on a screen. All this helps astronomers study the stars.

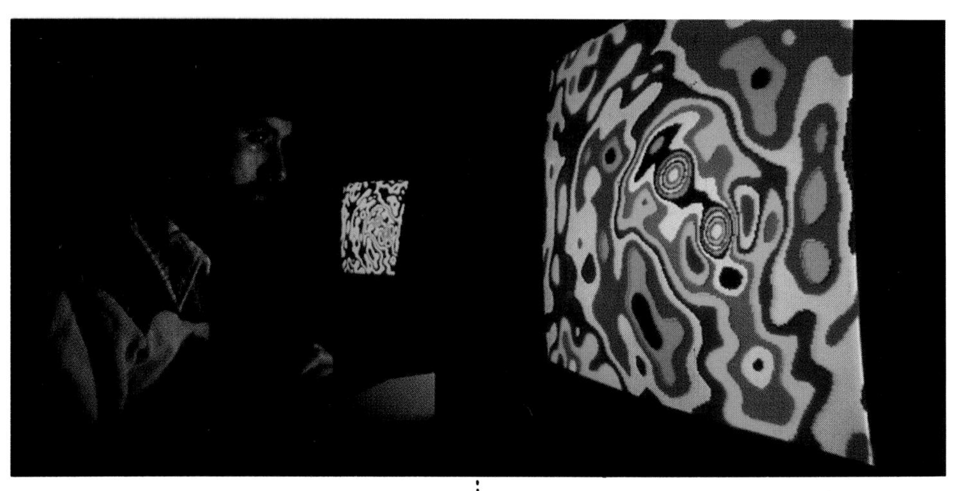

How can we best study the stars?

The best way to observe the stars is to get above the air. **Astronauts** travelling in space see the stars shining steadily. In space, stars do not twinkle! This is because space has no air. Without air, starlight travels straight through space without bending.

In 1990, scientists put the Hubble Space Telescope into orbit round the Earth. They hoped that the telescope would take clearer pictures of the stars. Unfortunately, the Hubble's mirror had a flaw which didn't allow astronomers to see the stars as well as they had hoped. But the telescope was fixed in 1993 and is now taking clearer pictures of stars than we can take from Earth.

More questions about the stars

Even though the twinkling of the stars is an optical illusion, it is still beautiful. We never tire of looking at the stars twinkling in the darkness, and we cannot help wondering more about them. How many stars exist? Are there different kinds of stars? Will we ever be able to travel to the stars? The questions we can ask about stars are almost as numerous as the stars themselves. Future astronomers will find even more questions to ask – and answer.

Glossary

astronaut: a person trained to fly spacecraft or who travels in a spacecraft

astronomer: a person who studies and observes the stars, the planets and other space objects

Hubble Space Telescope: the powerful telescope in orbit round the Earth which scientists hope will help them to see very distant stars and other space objects

laser: a device that gathers radiation and other types of energy and changes them into a powerful beam of light

optical illusion: anything that appears to be visible to the eye, but in fact is not real

star: a giant globe of gas that sends out light, heat and radiation into space

telescope: a device that uses lenses and mirrors to observe distant objects in space

twinkling: flickering and shimmering, as a star does in the night sky

Index